Moe Asch: A Speculative Life in Verse

And Other Poems

Moe Asch: A Speculative Life in Verse

And Other Poems

by

Benjamin Goluboff

© 2025 Benjamin Goluboff. All rights reserved.
This material may not be reproduced in any form, published,
reprinted, recorded, performed, broadcast,
rewritten or redistributed without
the explicit permission of Benjamin Goluboff.
All such actions are strictly prohibited by law.

Cover design by Shay Culligan
Cover image "Moses Asch in his Folkways Records Office
in New York City" by James Capaldi, available
through a Creative Commons license

ISBN: 978-1-63980-825-0
Library of Congress Control Number: 2025950380

Kelsay Books
502 South 1040 East, A-119
American Fork, Utah 84003
Kelsaybooks.com

for Catherine

Acknowledgements

Some of the poems in this volume appeared in the following journals and anthologies; grateful acknowledgment to their editors and staff.

45th Parallel: "Bronzeville Manifests in the Studio as Moe Asch Records Gwendolyn Brooks Reading 'Kitchenette Building'"
Abstract Magazine: "THICH"
The Al Magre Review: "Environmental Studies"
Chicago Literati: "Profiles Theater Shuttered, June 8, 2016"
The Contemporary Poetry series of Corbel Stone Press: "George Perkins Marsh on the Anthropogenic Dispersion of Seeds"
The Cordite Poetry Review: "President Donald J. Trump at the Western Wall, Jerusalem, 2017"
Dunes Review: "Couple-Shtick"
Elevation Review: "National Prose Month," "Zen and the Music of Earth Wind and Fire"
Fourth River: "Guerrilla Gardening; Chicago, North Side"
Maintenant, A Journal of Contemporary Dada Writing and Art: "More Archaic Torso"
Misfit Magazine: "Culture Clash at the Sausage Factory," "Mr. Peale's Illustrious Sons"
Mizmor Ha David annual of Poetica Press: "In the Hebrew Cemetery of Sheboygan"
Red Earth Review: "Green Men"
Share: "Truc Lam Temple Closed and Tagged," "Googling the Dead"
Sheila-Na-Gig: "Chicago Corners," "Bike Nocturne," "Liu Dan, 'The Dictionary,' 1991. Ink and Watercolor on Paper"
The Stay Project: "The Fraying of the Flag"
Stoneboat: "Minor White in Love"
Taint Taint Taint: "Moe Asch Records Sterling Brown Reading 'Ma Rainey' and is Deceived. Early 1940s"

Third Wednesday: "Moe Asch Declares Bankruptcy, 1948"
Triggerfish Critical Review: "On a Church Steeple in Scaffolding,"
  "On the Persistence of the Self"
*Vending Machine Pres*s: *"Cena Trimalchionis"*

Contents

Author's Note   13

I. Moe Asch: A Speculative Life in Verse

Moe Asch Builds Mansions   17
Moe Asch Orders Delivery   18
Moe Asch Installs the Transmitter for the
   New WEVD   19
Moe and Frances Asch Go to a Party, circa 1944   24
Moe Asch Records Sterling Brown Reading
   "Ma Rainey" and Is Deceived, Early 1940s   27
Moe Asch Records Mary Lou Williams and Her Six
   Performing "Gjon Mili Jam Session," June 5, 1944   30
Moe Asch in the Tabloids   32
Moe Asch Declares Bankruptcy, 1948   35
Moe Asch Checks Room Tone, Early 1950s   36
Bronzeville Manifests in the Studio as Moe Asch
   Records Gwendolyn Brooks Reading "Kitchenette
   Building," 1954   37
Moe Asch Records Nathan "Prince" Nazaroff
   Performing "Tumbalalaika" and Reflects on Not
   Knowing Yiddish, 1954   38
Moe Asch Records John Cage Performing "Dance"
   for Folkways *Sounds of New Music* (Various Artists),
   Released 1957   41
Interlude: Three Folkways Albums with Art by
   Ben Shahn   42
A Passage in Peter D. Goldsmith's Biography of
   Moe Asch   43

A Neighbor in Daisy, Kentucky, Recalls Roscoe Holcomb's Account of His Meetings in Manhattan with Moe Asch	44
Moe Asch Interviews W.E.B. DuBois, 1961, (Folkways Records FW05511)	47
Moe Asch Records Flat	49
Moe Asch Reviews the Master for The Fugs' First Album and Has Buyer's Remorse	50
Bob Dylan Is an Area of Darkness in the Mind of Moe Asch, 1970s	52
Interviewed in 1978, Moe Asch Remembers Woody Guthrie	54
In Old Age Moe Asch Thinks About Folk Music and Gets Pissed Off	56

II. Eight Portraits by G.P.A. Healy

John James Audubon, 1838	61
Andrew Jackson, 1845	63
Webster's Reply to Hayne, 1851	64
Nathaniel Hawthorne, 1852	65
Father Edward Taylor, Seamen's Apostle, 1855	67
Eleanor Boyle Ewing Sherman, 1868	69
Franz Liszt, 1869	72
Louisa May Alcott, 1870	74

III. Chicagoland, Arts & Letters, Other

Bike Nocturne	77
Chicago Corners	78

THICH	79
Guerrilla Gardening: Chicago, North Side	80
The Water Tower in All Lights and Weathers	82
Chicago Bikers	83
Scene From the Pandemic	85
On a Steeple in Scaffolding	86
Cena Trimalchionis	87
President Donald J. Trump at the Western Wall, Jerusalem, 2017	88
The Fraying of the Flag	90
Culture Clash at the Sausage Factory	91
Profiles Theater Shuttered, June 8, 2016	92
Truc Lam Temple Closed and Tagged	93
Zen and the Music of Earth Wind and Fire	95
Minor White in Love	96
Mr. Peale's Illustrious Sons	97
More Archaic Torso	99
Environmental Studies	100
George Perkins Marsh on the Anthropogenic Dispersion of Seed	101
Green Men	102
Marked Animals	103
Googling the Dead	104
National Prose Month	105
In the Hebrew Cemetery of Sheboygan	106
Couple-Shtick	108
On the Persistence of the Self	109
Glossary of Yiddish Terms	111

Author's Note

American record executive Moses Asch (1905–1986) built an encyclopedic catalog of world music through commercial labels including Asch, Disc, and Folkways.

Son of the controversial Yiddish-language writer Sholem Asch, Moe trained as an electrical engineer in Germany during Hitler's early rise to power. In a recording career that crossed decades, Asch captured something of the global variety of people's music. Folkways records were particularly beloved by the listeners and musicians of the 1960s folk music revival. The entire Folkways catalog is now in the care of the Smithsonian Institute and readily searchable on the internet.

Notwithstanding some palliative language from Tiny Robinson, Leadbelly's niece, interviewed for a Smithsonian podcast, Asch is generally remembered as having subjected the artists he recorded to unfair business practices. He is the subject of a brilliant biography by Peter D. Goldsmith.

I. Moe Asch: A Speculative Life in Verse

Moe Asch Builds Mansions

The first time he heard the gospel verse
about my father's house has many mansions,
he was so young it would have been in French,
or maybe Polish, but he would always remember thinking
that first time: well yes, my father's too.

The mansions of little Moishe's father
—*Tateleh,* glamorous and absent—
sat on *tante* Basha's shelf,
apart from the other books,
each, he would know it better as he grew,
a little world with people and weather
and history of its own:
a mansion in the house.

And as Moe grew,
from year to year and house to house,
the question grew inside him:
What mansions will I build?

Moe Asch Orders Delivery

The order was for the whitefish special
on black bread,
and two fried chickens,
so I was wondering who the mastermind was
behind that.

This is 1942,
my last year at P.S. Whatever,
just before I went into the service,
and the order is for an office in
the old WEVD building
on 46th.

There's just two people there:
a Jew, big sloppy loud-talking guy,
who does not tip me, by the way,
and this Black guy, very smartly dressed.

The Jew is looking for his wallet,
yelling at somebody over the phone,
"You people are going to put me out of business,"
and the Black guy is peeling an apple
with a very serious knife.

It wasn't until the sixties,
when everyone was
listening to that stuff
that I figured out
who the Black guy was.

Moe Asch Installs the Transmitter for the New WEVD

When in 1932 *The Jewish Daily Forward,*
under Abraham Cahan, took over
New York City's socialist radio station, WEVD
(named for Eugene V. Debs
and 1300 on your AM dial)
it was not entirely a matter of nepotism
that the contract for building the new transmitter
and installing a new antenna on the roof
of a mid-rise office building
in the Theater District, 46th and 7th,
should go to Moses Asch,
son of the celebrated Yiddish-language novelist
and beloved *Forward* columnist, Sholem Asch.

Labor leader and *Forward* manager
Baruch Charney Vladeck
knew the young man's mettle,
and was an effective advocate for him with Cahan.
Also Moe's little *gesheft,* Radio Labs,
was getting to be in demand
as the city's Jewish community
showed itself willing,
even in the Depression,
to acquire the new audio technologies
that were transforming lives across the nation.
By the time Moe signed the contract with Cahan
Radio Labs had installed public address systems
in Minsky's Burlesque on Lafayette,

Schwartz's Yiddish Art Theater,
2nd Avenue and 12th,
and three sleepaway camps in the Catskills.
In '36 Moe would wire the Polo Grounds
for the May Day rally of the International
Ladies' Garment Workers Union.

The antenna was to be sited
on the building's roof next to a little utility shed
behind the street-side facade,
and Moe went up there that fall
to inspect the site with the building engineer,
a peculiar elderly *frummer* who made the young man
carry an ashcan, shovel, and broom
up the last flight of stairs from the freight elevator
to the roof hatch because, he said,
sounding like a stage Yid from Minsky's,
you never know what you're going to find
when you open these things.

And just as the guy predicted,
when they opened the shed,
they discovered the floor of the place,
and the cast-off rubbish inside,
to be covered with a varied frosting of birdshit,
and littered with the delicately articulated skeletons
of a dozen pigeons, and with the bits and bones
of assorted smaller creatures:
the aerie, they had uncovered,
the banqueting-room of the midtown
Peregrine Falcon.

While Moe, a person of queasy stomach,
walks away to the windward side of the roof,
to watch the sundown skyline,
and the *frummer* shovels out the dead birds,
we may remark that the young man
(just now on the cusp of a mountaintop experience),
was about to set in motion a controversy
that would trouble New Yorkers for decades.
Yiddish on the radio was no novelty,
although it was unwelcome to some,
but *The Forward's* takeover of WEVD
exposed all the old ethnic divisions
in the party's universalist platform
that the socialists had been arguing about
for fifty years on two continents.

And while some loyal listeners
variously considered the new programming
to be a dulling of the old station's ideological edge,
a desertion of the trade unionists,
a betrayal of the principles of Mr. Debs himself,
others—many of them Jews—took WEVD to their hearts,
as they had taken Cahan's *Forward* itself,
would enshrine it in their memories of the ghetto cocoon,
of *Yiddishkeit* and *mamaloshen*.

Stormy, mercurial, animated by contradictions
that would disable any other man
(socialist-entrepreneur, assimilator-apologist)
Abraham Cahan, the Ahab of American writers,
had built in *The Forward* an instrument of astonishing power.

It would be devastating, ten years after the transmitter was running,
when Cahan broke, decisively and vindictively, with Moe's father,
when Sholem became a scandal once more.

Now, 1932, Moe stands at the parapet
looking north toward Radio City
as the Manhattan workday winds down,
and he has fallen into a reverie.
Ever since he built his first ham set,
Moe had delighted in radio's power and reach.
Tonight, surveying the rooftops,
he imagined radio as a bird of prey
soaring from the parapet
owning the space above the five boroughs,
the blocks above the blocks,
occupying that birds-eye vertiginous perspective
from which abstractions like neighborhood,
guild, or nation, become spatial and flat.

The young man would have gone on
to dream of the falcon's agency
in distributing culture and forming community,
but he was interrupted by a sound
that provoked in him a wild surmise.
Or sound, perhaps, is not the word
for this something Moe detected
among the noises of the five-o-clock city,
framing and informing those noises
as in a visual composition negative space
frames and informs the outline of its subject.

This something was associated,
in the young man's mind, with the coming night,
yet was not coextensive with the night,
was participant in the night,
inflected and conditioned the night,
yet retained being-for-itself apart from the night.
It became clear to Moe after a few moments,
and in this clarity he would be guided and ennobled.
On the roof of what came to be called the WEVD building,
Moe Asch heard America listening.

Moe and Frances Asch Go to a Party, circa 1944

Lead Belly's apartment was wonderful . . . it was the best damn hootenanny that ever took place . . . everybody was there, all the people who later would acquire halos and legends were there.
—Frederic Ramsey

Was that Walter Lippman
making out in the shower stall
with one of the NYU coeds,
or was it the economist
from the New School
with the German accent
who had been lecturing,
a moment ago in the kitchen,
about the Molotov-Ribbentrop pact
to a couple of sailors who,
hearing the ruckus from the street,
had climbed Lead's stairs
and invited themselves in?

Moe, peeing, tried not to look,
then made his way back to Frances,
—sane, plain, sensible Frances—
who had become suddenly
and bottomlessly drunk
on what had seemed
just a thimbleful
of Martha Promise's corn liquor,
and could not now be stopped
from making corny jokes like:
"Martha promises
and, boy, does she deliver!"

And Lead sang:
You folks are my best,
I'll sing your request.

Everyone was saying
how Langston Hughes
had been there earlier
in the evening.
Sonny Terry and Brownie McGhee
were leading some kind of
jump or breakdown
in the living room.
(Moe hadn't heard it before
and made a mental note.)
And of course Woody was there,
twangin' and opinin'
dropping folk wisdom
like a leaky bucket,
going around the party
trying out rhymes on the people:
"porridge" and "carriage,"
whaddaya think?
"Secular" and "regular?"

And Lead sang:
You folks are mine,
I'll sing for you fine.

And there, flowering by the wall,
rapt like a pilgrim at a shrine,
stood Peggy Guggenheim.
Poor little rich girl,
thwarted and patronized,
recently deserted
by Max Ernst,
(that preening ass)
Peggy burned,
let it be remembered,
with a hard and gem-like flame.
She had sampled
all the waters of Bohemia,
and Peggy knew that here,
414 E. 10th St.,
she had found the true,
the blushful Hippocrene.

And Lead sang:
You make me feel new,
I'll sing best for you.

Moe Asch Records Sterling Brown Reading "Ma Rainey" and Is Deceived, Early 1940s

Moe had mixed feelings.
He was put off, for starters,
by Brown's use of dialect,
knowing, or believing he knew,
how the contractions
and elisions would sound
to younger urban Blacks.

And then there was
the misattribution to Ma
—stunning, really—
of whole lines
from Bessie Smith's
"Back-Water Blues,"
lines most certainly
under copyright
to some fortunate
third party, if not to
the gods of Columbia
themselves—
lines reproduced here
all but verbatim.

But he was at the same time charmed
by the tenor of Brown's tenor
as it visited all the stations of a prosody
that, Moe knew, owed more
to Northern-European verse traditions

than to the Afro-Caribbean forms
in which the poet's ancestors sang.

And for reasons associated
with his historical moment,
cultural milieu,
and professional vocation,
Moe was susceptible
to the force of the poem's
central conceit:
that there is one voice
that speaks for us all,
that just gets hold of us
somekindaway.

Moe's way was to shed,
in spite of himself,
a single stingy tear
for Brown's Ma.

And here, sadly,
Moe was deceived.
Ma sang for the people
in the poet's song,
gave voice to their
aspirations and miseries,
but Ma and the record executive
lived outside of the song
and occupied

—for reasons not only of race
but of ontological necessity—
realities disjunct
and incommunicable.
It was a lie
to pretend otherwise,
a lie to shed
the single tear.
For who was Ma to Moe,
or Moe to Ma,
that he should
weep for her?

Moe Asch Records Mary Lou Williams and Her Six Performing "Gjon Mili Jam Session," June 5, 1944

Now this was very advanced stuff for the forties,
very out-there, very *outré,* very future.
The rhythm section, Al Lucas and Jack Parker,
are exploring one of the identities
from Ramanujan's notebooks,
while the reed men, Claude Greene and Don Byas
are having a crack at Fermat's last theorem.
Big Vic Dickenson on trombone
is performing an autopsy
on Schrödinger's cat,
while on the trumpet
Mr. Dick Vance is giving
the cat a saucer of milk.

Mary supports them all.
She responds, she affirms,
she does not make it about herself,
sometimes asserts a riff or phrase
like a shark breaking the surface
then going under again.
Or maybe this is just the way,
out of some misguided notion
of equity or flatness,
Moe has mic'd the session.

The title of the composition
refers to an event held in the year previous
to the Asch recording
at the studio of *Life* photographer, Gjon Mili,
who loved jazz and its players,
and whom the jazz world loved right back.

Moe Asch in the Tabloids

*"Offbeat," Time Magazine, 2 Feb. 1946,
Vol. 47, Issue 8, p. 65.*

. . . Moe (for Moses) Asch, 40,
has become the nation's
No. 1 recorder of
out-of-the-way jazz,
cowboy music,
and such exotic items
as Paris street noises
during the liberation,
and little-heard Russian operas.

Last week Moe Asch
hit the market
with ten albums
(under the new label of Disc)
which included such
typically offbeat items
as Trinidad Calypsos
by "Lord (Rum & Coca-Cola) Invader,"
new 'sinful' songs
by the Negro ex-convict Leadbelly,
a newly famed jazz trio
playing Harlem blues
and a Creole lullaby,
mandolinist Bess Lomax
singing Careless Love
("now my apron strings won't pin"),

four French Resistance fighters
reading their own poems
and editorials.

Asch, whose studio
is a cluttered room
in Manhattan's drab
WEVD building,
has almost a fear of hits,
and he brushes off
commercial jazz
as if it were
an unmentionable
disease.

. . . Asch calls his albums
"basic music"
to distinguish them
from popular swing
or the Gene Autry-Bob Willis,
(*Time*, Feb 11) kind of folk music.
Said he: 'Ours get down
to the musical roots.
Very often a basic song
like Buffalo Gals
("Can't you come out tonight?")

becomes a hit,
but I'm not interested
in individual hits.
To me a catalogue
of folk expression
is the most important thing.'

. . . as soon as he can,
Asch hopes to record folk music
from the southern Soviet republics
of Tadjik and Azerbaijan,
Greece, Hungary,
South Africa and Haiti.
Says he: "It's not profitable,
but it's steady."

Moe Asch Declares Bankruptcy, 1948

It was so cold the winter Moe went bankrupt
that the crows congealed in the skies above Manhattan,
fell to earth and shattered
in glassy black fragments on the avenues.
Children stood with their tongues
stuck to utility poles,
patiently waiting for spring,
and the East River froze solid.

Tears made a mask of rime on Moe's face,
as he carried the business across the ice,
brick by brick, master by master,
reincorporating on the far side
in the name of his secretary,
and sometime mistress,
Marian Distler.

Moe Asch Checks Room Tone, Early 1950s

Bronzeville Manifests in the Studio as Moe Asch Records Gwendolyn Brooks Reading "Kitchenette Building," 1954

A Buick Skylark, robin's-egg blue,
rolled up to Moe's console
and out of its open windows,
along with some pungent smoke,
came a blues in stop-time arrangement:
the latest thing from Chess Records.
Kids were yelling something like,
"Snatch it back and hold it,"
or yelling whatever kids were yelling
at 31st and Prairie at that particular time.
Little girl come off
the playground slide funny,
skinned the heel of her hand,
ran home crying.

Moe Asch Records Nathan "Prince" Nazaroff Performing "Tumbalalaika" and Reflects on Not Knowing Yiddish, 1954

Except for the guy's whistling,
which was uncanny,
the Prince was no great shakes
as a musician, but musicianship
was never the main point for Moe.
And Nazaroff turned out to be a trouper,
getting through the ten sides
of *Jewish Freilach Songs*
each in a single take,
except for "Tumbalalaika,"
where the guy got all *farklempt*
and had to start over.

Setting up for the re-take,
Moe was happy to feel himself immune
to the song's power.
He knew it was something
about maidens and gypsies and springtime,
knew it was associated
in the minds of American Jews
with a European past
now all but illegible,
but was pleased to recognize
that "Tumbalalaika" put no mist
whatsoever on his windshield.

People thought it was funny
that the son of Sholem Asch
couldn't speak Yiddish,
but Moe knew there were advantages.
It was, for one thing, a free pass
out of at least some of the dreary, mawkish,
bagels-and-lox nostalgia
that was the dominant note
in American-Jewish conversation in those years.
Absurd: the *alrightniks* pining for the *shtetl*.
Well, the *alrightniks* could have Nazaroff.

None of Sholem's children knew Yiddish,
except for Ruthie, the youngest,
who had learned deliberately
from a tutor in adult life.
And Moe's grip on language in general
was always a little uncertain,
his critical years for language acquisition
having passed during the family's refugee journey
from Slavic to Romance to New Yawk.
Moe's English, people would remember,
was confused, a blunt instrument,
slow-moving and maladroit.

Sholem always said it didn't matter to him
if the children learned Yiddish or not,
and this was consistent with Sholem's views
about everything involving the children,
as long as they stayed quiet when under his roof.

Moe had known his father's writing
mainly from the reverb
(some of it *sturm,* the rest *drang*)
that it made upon the wider world,
had read what he'd read of it
only in the English of Maurice Samuel,
or the English-by-way-of-German
of Willa and Edwin Muir.

And Moe had read the translations
with the dawning certainty
that Sholem had been more deliberate
than he seemed in making Yiddish
an undiscovered country for his children.
Moe had come to believe
there was some part of his father's soul
Sholem wished to keep hidden from them.

Moe Asch Records John Cage Performing "Dance" for Folkways *Sounds of New Music* (Various Artists), Released 1957

Imagine him levitating
an inch and a half above his chair,
seized with fierce aesthetic emotion,
as Mr. Cage's prepared Steinway
goes thunkety-thunk-thunking along.

Interlude: Three Folkways Albums with Art by Ben Shahn

The angel on the cover of Folkways 1953
Gospel Songs Sung by the Missionary Quintet
blows a transparent horn before a block of text,
hand-lettered *(con brio)* from Psalms 150.[1]

Shahn's working men hide their faces:
the pen-and-ink guitarist on Folkways
Cowboy Ballads Sung by Cisco Houston with Guitar,
1952, weeps into the crook of his arm

like the fellow reclining on *Smoky Mt. Ballads
Sung by Bascom Lamar Lunsford with Banjo,*
as if on a porch up there in the high and lonesome,
who lays a forearm across his eyes.

---

[1] *The finest of Shahn's angels was done not for Folkways, but for the 1964 Columbia recording (ML 5042) of Albert Schweitzer playing a repertoire of organ music by J.S. Bach. Here Shahn's angel, his wings in disarray, looks heavenward from the keys of a foreshortened instrument with a look of fierce determination on his blocky upturned face.*

A Passage in Peter D. Goldsmith's Biography of Moe Asch

On page 278
in 1957
Odetta is
leaving
117 W. 46th St.
as Ella Jenkins
is coming in
and Odetta
says to Ella:
"Make sure you
get some royalties."

A Neighbor in Daisy, Kentucky, Recalls Roscoe Holcomb's Account of His Meetings in Manhattan with Moe Asch

Every few years starting in 19 and 61
the Friends of Old Time Music
(some sort of longhair front organization,
you can bet) would bring Roscoe
down from Daisy to New York's town
to play in one of them beatnik halls
for the campus kids and the girls,
to hear Roscoe tell it, in black nylons.

The New Yorkers called his music folk,
which was a puzzle to Roscoe,
who said it made about as much sense
as calling folks music.
Roscoe sang the church tunes
from the Old Regular Baptist outfit,
the ballads and story-songs
of our cracker forebears,
and some of the Negro music
for which people up here
use an impolite name.

Roscoe said he liked the city,
even though it scared him a little,
and I figure that was because
they treated him like a big shot there.
After the shows, he told us,
they used to bring him around

to the big man who made the records,
who was a Jew or Jewish fellow
named Moses,
and this tickled Roscoe,
who had only met
a Jewish fellow once before,
and that was the kid
in the Studebaker
drove up here
said he was looking
for banjo players.

Roscoe said Moses always
gave him an LP with the songs
from Roscoe's last visit to the Friends
and a crisp new 50-dollar bill.
Said he and Moses used to cut up
there in the studio and have a fine time.
Said he wrote Moses letters over the years
and that Moses, or his secretary,
always wrote back politely.
Said Moses was a good fellow
even if he was a Jew.

Now I believe Roscoe knew
he was being cheated.
It was only he was so broken down,

from the mining and the millwork,
that by the time the Jews found him
he didn't much care anymore.

Moe Asch Interviews W.E.B. DuBois, 1961, (Folkways Records FW05511)

. . . Now on the other hand
I go down to Fisk University and
suddenly I am in a Negro world where
all the people except the teachers
(and the teachers in their thought
and action) belong to this colored
world and the world was almost complete. I mean, we acted and thought
as people belonging to this group.
And I got the idea that my work was
in that group. That while I was, in
the long run, going to try to break
down segregation and separateness,
yet for the time I was quite willing
to be a Negro and to work within a
Negro group. Now I came from there
to Harvard and there was a change
and yet I met it in a peculiar sort
of way. I mean, if I'd gone directly from my high school in Great
Barrington to Harvard, I would've
thought of myself as a Massachusetts
man and my fellows would've been
the whites there. But coming back
from Fisk I brought with me the feeling of a separate race. I never
felt myself a Harvard man as I'd

felt myself a Fisk man. I was coming to Harvard for a particular purpose—to try to carry further the education that I'd received at Fisk, but to work by myself, to seek no contact with my fellows. If they wanted to know me they had to make the effort on their part. So out of that class of 300 I don't suppose I knew 10 really, intimitally [sic] at all.

Moe Asch Records Flat

Right up until the end of the fifties
when he started farming out
the studio work to Mel Kaiser at Cue,
Moe insisted on only recording flat:
one mic placed brilliantly,
and everybody finds
his level around it.
It was like he thought
the mixing board
made some kind of *treyf.*

Talk to him about
Phil Spector and the Wall of Sound,
and Moe would spit on the floor
like he was a *Europsche* peasant,
and you had said something
to call down the Evil Eye.

Moe Asch Reviews the Master for The Fugs' First Album and Has Buyer's Remorse

Under the sign of Coyote
or trickster Loki
came record producer
and freak Harry Smith
to Moe and sold him
on the band named,
for what Mailer called
you-know-what.

Moe thought he could
see the guy's point,
drew up a contract,
sent Harry and the Fugs
down to Mel Kaiser,
but it wasn't until
he listened to the master
for the 1965 release
that Moe realized
the enormity
of what he'd done.

Rock and Roll was Caliban,
Moe understood,
but this was something else
for which he had no name.
(The Fugs, of course,
were nobody's folk.)

And when Tuli and Ed
and the rest of them
tried to harmonize on
"How Sweet I Roamed
from Field to Field,"
Moe heard William Blake
weeping.

Bob Dylan Is an Area of Darkness in the Mind of Moe Asch, 1970s

. . . a zone of taboo interference,
a site of trauma and obsessive return.
Dear loving Frances understood
this about her husband,
called it his *Dylanschmertz*
and watched patiently nights
as Moe paced the floor
in its grip.

It wasn't just the money
the kid was making for Columbia
(bushels and bags of glistening coin).
And it wasn't just resentment
about how John Hammond
(that smug aristo prick)
had renovated his cult of personality
through the kid.

Neither was it entirely about the kid's music,
which looped and perseverated
in Moe's sleepless head:
so unlike the real thing and so like,
so balanced on a knife edge
(Moe felt it beneath his old-man ugly feet)
one side of which
was nonsense.

No, Moe's *Dylanschmertz* had two
deep sources, neither of which
had become articulate
in the record executive's conscious mind.
One was an uncanny dread about
how the kid, like the repressed returning, had made
himself the *doppelganger* of poor, dead, burned
doomed Woody.

The other lay hidden behind
Moe's recognition that the Zimmerman kid
embodied the first motif of folk narrative:
a young man leaves the small town
to make his fortune in the city.
With the crazy eyes and *farshimmelt* hair
the kid could have been a character in one of
Sholem's stories.

Young Sholem had left Kutno for Warsaw
where the world awaited him,
like Woody left Dustville Oklahoma,
and stepped, poor clown, into history.
All of this affected Moe with a generalized
dread about his own mortality.
For Moe was an old man then,
long settled in the city.

Interviewed in 1978, Moe Asch Remembers Woody Guthrie

Bluestein, Gene. "Moses Asch, Documentor." *American Music*, vol. 5, no.3, 1987, pp. 291–304.

In his own way
Woody was the most
antisocial person I ever met.
He didn't like people,
especially middle-class
bourgeois people.
When he came to New York
he didn't meet people
of his own kind,
his own background.
But he had a driving force
and a knowledge
of what he stood for.

He felt that he represented
a group of poor people
that needed to be spoken for,
and he wanted to
give them exposure.

When you talked to Woody
he behaved like a hippie
—that's the closest word.
He would sit on the floor,
he'd look in one direction
and say a couple of words,
that's all; then he'd go home

and write me a beautiful, long letter,
more lucid than his talking.
He was a terrific writer.

As long as I didn't bother him
and contradict him
but listened to him
and used his idea,
he felt comfortable with me.

. . . he was using me
like a pen, to make a book.
I was working the machinery,
but he was using it for himself.

I never looked at his hair,
his way of dressing.
That was Woody,
you accepted Woody
the way he was.

In Old Age Moe Asch Thinks About Folk Music and Gets Pissed Off

Near the end, Moe was angry a lot of the time,
even though it wasn't always clear why.
Dave Van Ronk saw a lot of angry Moe,
as did good, patient Frances.
Marian Distler, long since
gone beneath the waves,
could have taken them all to school
about the record executive's angers,
but silence was Marian's portion now.
Sometimes late at night, his candle sputtering,
Moe believed his angers were the only thing
keeping him alive.

He was angry (ironic laughter)
about the commodification of the music:
the Rock people cashing in on it,
Izzy Young making it retail on MacDougal St.
He was angry about the disconnect
between the music and its population of origin:
the proletariat, persistent and indisputable,
who listened, Moe knew, in their tenements
and tar-paper shacks, to Tin Pan Alley *chazerei*,
to the Captain (Moe's entrails writhed) and Tenille.

And he was angry about the puritanism
of the folkies with their cult of authenticity,
the jesuitical parsing and unparsing
of the Real Thing with the Real Presence,

the collectors and ethnomusicologists
fanning out across the hills and hollows,
infiltrating the rural poor, looking for dead shellac
and geriatric players like knights errant
looking for slivers of the True Cross:
John Cohen who discovered St. Roscoe,
Harry Smith, that lowlife grifter freak
—all of them *en train* to Lomax *pére,*
that cowboy fantasist, who was just as bad
as Lomax *fils,* litigious son of a bitch,
who needed those copyrights
like a fiend needs fix.

But the rich creamy center of Moe's anger
was reserved for Pete Seeger who, you will recall,
deserted Moe in 1964 after Columbia Records
took him up to a high place
and showed him the kingdoms of the earth.
Meek and mild Pete. St. Authentic.
The *putz* who tried to unplug the Zimmerman kid
when he did that thing at Newport in '65.
Mr. Rectitude. Mr. Integrity.
The squeaky-clean predestined One
in whom New Left and Old Left are reconciled.
World without end. *Shantih, Shantih, Shantih.*
Pete Seeger. *Feh.*

At this little glow Moe warmed his hands
until it too was extinguished.

II. Eight Portraits by G.P.A. Healy

American portraitist George Peter Alexander Healy (1813–1894) was born in Boston, trained in the Paris atelier of Antoine-Jean Gros, and in 1855 chose Chicago as adoptive home and base of operations. Following commissions over a prodigious career, Healy may have crossed the Atlantic more frequently than anyone of his generation besides professional mariners. His sitters included statesmen and royalty, writers and soldiers, Pope Pius IX, Abraham Lincoln, and Jenny Lind. Hundreds of Healy's paintings were lost in the Chicago fire; hundreds more survive around the world, including a collection at Chicago's Newberry Library. Healy tells some of his story in *Reminiscences of a Portrait Painter* (1894). I am indebted to Edward N. Waters' "Liszt and Longfellow," *The Musical Quarterly*, 41:1 (1955), pp. 1–25, and to Frederick Voss's "Webster Replying to Hayne: George Healy and the Economics of History Painting," *American Art*, 15:1 (2001), pp. 34–53.

John James Audubon, 1838

Healy painted Audubon
when the ornithologist was 53
and the painter 25.
The portrait is a young man's work,
Healy's dashing technique
as much the subject of the composition
as the naturalist himself.
Healy puts decorative stitching
on Audubon's bandolier and game bag
with the *elan* he might have brought
to a young lady's bouquet
or a matron's needlework.

On the trilliums that bloom
in the bosky shade
where the naturalist reclines,
head on hand
against a dead allegorical branch,
Healy lavishes such precision
that he must have believed himself
to be painting in competition
with his sitter, who,
unknown to the young man,
delegated the botanicals,
uncredited, to his assistant,
Joseph Mason.
In the contrast he draws
between Audubon's loose white shirt,
open romantically at the collar,
and the naturalist's sun-bronzed skin,

Healy brushes up a little parable
of the American frontier.

Except for the long straight nose,
Audubon, who must have been
a twitchy sitter, looks like a different man
in every portrait made of him.
In the study by the ornithologist's son,
done just a few years after Healy's portrait,
the father's face is blocky and expressionless,
as if John Woodhouse had trouble
seeing John James clearly.
In John Syme's portrait,
made just a few years prior to Healy's,
Audubon, wearing his signature buckskins,
is pallid and narrow-faced
and wears an expression
of surprise, perhaps affront,
as he gazes upon some high purpose.

Healy's Audubon,
who looks very directly at the viewer,
is full-faced and well-fed,
robust and full of blood.
There is something of Falstaff here,
or something Dionysian.
It is as if below the composition,
outside of the frame,
Audubon's legs ended in hooves.

Andrew Jackson, 1845

In the final month of his illness the General,
unable to lie down without great pain,
sat sleepless in his armchair,
and denied the portraitist's request
when Healy presented the letter from Louis Phillipe:
"Can't sit, sir. Can't sit for all the kings in Christendom."
The General's daughter-in-law prevailed with him, however,
and Healy painted him in the armchair,
finished the portrait in a little more than a week,
was in the room for the old man's exit.
Framed close and rendered with minute realism,
Jackson's face in the portrait is a horror.

Webster's Reply to Hayne, 1851

The painting, which hangs in Boston's Faneuil Hall
and is set in the U.S. Senate chamber,
includes 130 likenesses made from engravings,
daguerreotypes, prior oil portraits,
or in a few instances live sittings.
Mainly these are of men and women
who were present at the 1830 event,
the memory of which had taken on
new urgency as the nation
lapsed toward civil war.

Several others were introduced
by Healy for his own reasons.
One of these, just a head in the spectator's gallery,
is the painter Thomas Couture, Healy's *copain,*
to whose "Romans of the Decadence"
the contemporary press often compared
"Webster's Reply."
Another is Alexis de Tocqueville
who in fact did not begin his tour
of the United States until the year following
the Webster—Hayne debate,
but whom Healy wished to imagine
as taking it all in.

Nathaniel Hawthorne, 1852

Healy's account of Hawthorne's sittings
records the novelist's excessive timidity
and self-consciousness,
his inability to meet the portraitist's eye
without reddening and assuming
an expression of dismay.

New England in those days
being what New England was,
we know that at least one of them,
the painter or the novelist,
thought of Diana and Actaeon
and that for one of them at least
it would have been as if something improper
stood undraped in Healy's studio.

Nothing could dispel the cloud
of embarrassment in the little room
until Mrs. Healy offered to read aloud
from one of the novels of Bulwer.
This calmed Hawthorne, who
over the course of the sittings
became more at ease with George and Louisa,
eventually sharing with them anecdotes
from Sophia's and his early married life.

Sophia, custodian of the novelist's image,
never visited the studio
but had a hand in the portrait nonetheless.
The novelist's mustache

which figures in Healy's *Reminiscences*
and which from Sophia's perspective
tethered Hawthorne to his body,
did not make it to the canvas.

Father Edward Taylor, Seamen's Apostle, 1855

That portraiture has a rhetoric
Healy understood in the cartilage
and small bones of his hand.
Of rhetoricians as subjects
he had collected,
by the time Taylor sat to him,
the finest of his generation:
Webster, Clay, Guizot.
But can rhetoric itself be portrayed?
Can you paint a trope?

By the time he sat to Healy,
a trope is what Taylor had become:
a figure by which the Unitarians
forgave the Methodists
for being so very much of the people,
by which the British forgave the Yankees,
a little, their bland and cheerful uniformity.
One of the models for Melville's Father Mapple,
Taylor was metonym for native untutored eloquence.

Dickens heard Taylor preach on *Song of Solomon,* 8:5,
("Who is this coming up from the wilderness,
leaning on the arm of her beloved?")
and wrote about the sermon
using both direct quotation
and free indirect discourse.
Emerson, who considered Taylor
another Robert Burns,
wrote of his preaching:

"Everything dances and disappears
—changes, becomes its contrary—
in his sculpturing hands."
Whitman called Taylor
a perfect orator.

There is no nautical device
in Healy's portrait of Father Taylor;
the preacher is shown without his book.
Healy has brushed a few years off the man,
softening the creases that track along
the old mariner's face
in all the period descriptions of him.
A peculiar silence presides in the portrait.
The preacher's lips are closed,
his features are animated
by no intention to speak.
This is Taylor turned aside from his ministry,
the fires banked, the machinery paused.

Eleanor Boyle Ewing Sherman, 1868

She wears black
and stands emphatically alone,
a Penelope-nun.
The silver cross
on the sash at her waist
is the composition's
secondary focal point.

Ellen had eight children with Sherman,
over a marriage of almost forty years.
There were the long absences
that come with any military marriage.
There were betrayals disclosed
and betrayals that stayed hidden
and there was the one thing
he would not give her.

Her father the senator's ward,
her companion in the woods,
and on the carriage roads of childhood
before the childhood love seasoned
and became something else,
then seasoned again
when the first of the children came
and Sherman (Cump she called him)
first broke his vows.

In every season he withheld the thing
that came to matter most to her.
Cump would not join her church,
which was Senator Ewing's church,
which was the universal church.
Ellen laid siege to the General
for decades and could not
dislodge the man and for decades
Ellen struggled in her spirit
to resist the bitterness
this caused in her.

The siege made strategy of their love.
There were better years and worse.
There were years when Cump's absences
helped love breathe more freely,
but when their second son Tom
joined the Jesuits in 1878,
it put a crack in the family
Ellen thought there would be
no recovering from,
even if recovery, of a sort,
came at last.

Ellen died before the General,
but even in his grief,
which was deep and acute
and which roared in his ears like a barrage,
never mind the siege and the infidelities,
Sherman never once considered
joining the church.
When he was too far gone
on his deathbed
to do anything about it,
the children had a priest
give him last rites,
but Sherman cannot properly
be considered a convert.

It was easier for the Healys.
George just waited for Louisa
the first twenty-one years
of their marriage, until all the children
had undergone the Anglican catechism,
before the portraitist's wife took
the Roman Catholic eucharist with him.

Franz Liszt, 1869

The story goes
that Healy introduced
Henry Longfellow
to Liszt
when all of them
were in Rome
that New Year.
Liszt had taken
minor orders
and was in rooms
at Santa Francesca.
near the Forum
when he opened
the door
to the portraitist
and the poet.

You could say when Longfellow saw Liszt
he was a character in a Henry James novel
who sees in an instant
and with a terrible hollowness of spirit
everything his life had not been
because God or history
had not made him European.
Or you could say when Liszt opened the door,
the light of his candle fell upon Longfellow
he too saw a world that he had missed,
where creed and desire need not be at war,
where art could be delivered into being
by steady scholarly accumulation,
not in the orgies of renunciation
and its opposite that had been
Liszt's hard way.

The effect
was so striking
—framed in
the doorway
Liszt wears
clerical garb
and carries
a tall candle
that lights his face
from above—
that Longfellow
whispered:
"Oh Mr. Healy!
You must paint
that for me."
And Healy did.

Or you could say
that Liszt's candle
illuminated
nothing, finally,
that you can see clearly
from where you stand
in the onrushing present,
where you cling
like a straphanger
on the El to fictions
of progress and period
that simplify the record,
turn the mob into a parade,
and let you patronize
the people of the past
for not living when you live.

Louisa May Alcott, 1870

Many voices inhabited Miss Alcott:
the satirist, the pastoral elegist,
domestic melodramatist,
children's fabulist,
and anonymously,
or pseudonymously,
voices for the lurid,
the sensational,
and the gothic.

Interwoven with them all
was the voice of Bronson,
who spoke tirelessly
in Miss Alcott's head.

Healy was probably
not aware of these voices,
but he did see that something
had hurt Miss Alcott,
who gazes from the canvas
with a look of wounded
reproach.

III. Chicagoland, Arts & Letters, Other

Bike Nocturne

To speak ahead of the what and how
as the night blocks pass in streetlight,
to speak ahead of yourself
as your shadow, grey on the blacktop,
swings past you and again,
streetlight to streetlight,
swings past.

To speak like that.

To speak over your head and ahead of your grasp,
ahead of your shadow as it swings,
block to block, light to light,
ahead of your intention, even
ahead of your route.

Each route tonight an act of speech,
point to point in the city,
where the grid is our lexicon
and the lexicon our grid.

At Argyle and Glenwood
water runs loud beneath the street,
connecting distances in the dark.
Here are the range and inflections,
the reach of our idiom.

Chicago Corners

Ashland and Webster

Kids smoking weed
in the portico of a shuttered nightclub:
Green Dolphin Street.

Foster and Kenmore

The bass-line loud from a low-rider
makes strange harmony
with the music of the ice cream truck.

Lawrence and the River

End of the day and thunderheads to the north,
the woman puts padlock and chain
around the gates to the community garden.

Kedzie and Humboldt

People in wheelchairs line up
on the sidewalk by the clinic.
Someone's bumping T-Swift's "Shake it Off."

Milwaukee and Waveland

Sundown kindles the bricks
of the high school assembly building.
Maybe this is what you came for.

THICH

THICH was on top of 3240 W. Lawrence,
above where the granite says:
DAVID FIREPROOF STORAGE WAREHOUSE 1916,
which is above where the awning says:
L&L APPLIANCE MART.
This is between Kedzie and Sawyer,
across from TACO MONTANA
and GREAT SEA LOLLIPOP WINGS.
THICH was in pale green letters,
skinny tall letters on a background rollered black.
THICH faced west with a commanding view of Albany Park.
But someone got up there with stencils and paint,
just as spring was coming in this year,
and changed the tag to THICK.

Guerrilla Gardening: Chicago, North Side

When the city redid Lawrence Ave.,
widening the sidewalk and putting in a bike lane,
they cut wells in the pavement for rain gardens.
These would dampen the urban heat-island effect
and detain runoff from the downpours
expected with climate change.

The wells stayed empty all summer,
or would have, except the neighbors farmed them,
working the hard packed soil
that had lain sunless
beneath the concrete for most of a century.

At Cortes de Pelo Cut Color Style
they put in sweetcorn,
the Little Giant variety from Burpee.
It tasseled by the end of July
and bore moderately in the dog days.

At Restaurant Y Taqueria Primo Chuki's
it was Gulliver hybrid tomatillos
and okra, Clemson Spineless.
By the vape shop on Damen,
heirloom tomatoes and Siam Purple basil.

Next spring, as soon as the frost
was out of the ground,
the city planted the rain gardens with ornamentals,
and there was no more room for crops.

The Water Tower in All Lights and Weathers

If I were a painter I would spend all my time
at the corner of Foster and Pulaski
on the west end of Chicago's north side.
There I would paint the antique water tower
that rises in front of the crematorium
and says Bohemian National Cemetery.
This I would do in all lights and weathers,
but especially in the late mellow light
that falls from the south and west
at the end of the day, warming the greys
and brick-reds of my composition.

This light would warm the greens too
for I would also paint the uncut lawn
around the custodian's house,
the truck garden run to seed
by the disused conservatory,
the burdock squatting
by the old brick outbuilding.

Trampled earth, leaning grass,
the seed heads that grow
from weed flowers—
I would paint it all:
the whole transitional,
vernacular,
messily amalgamated,
polyglot thing.

Chicago Bikers

We fear no CTA bus for they are driven
by professionals, but we fear.

Crossing the river at Lawrence we fear,
we fear on Lower Wacker Drive.

Once I rode with these kids into traffic
I should have stayed out of,

and when I said to them afterwards,
"you guys are fearless,"

the alpha kid said, "no,
we got some fear."

On our fear we are trued and balanced,
by our fear we speed.

We whistle past the ghost bike
at Damen and Addison,

the ghost bike at Kedzie and Armitage,
the ghost bike at Pulaski and Diversey.

Still we roll or balance
still at the red light.

Sticker on the helmet,
HiVis saturated black,

Chance on random on blast
on the BlueTooth.

We try to make eye contact with you;
our doubt is your benefit still.

We are slow-rolling here about
our little clause in the social contract.

Scene From the Pandemic

Chinatown's First Sip Cafe,
Argyle and Kenmore,
has been closed since before
Shelter-in-Place began.
When they locked down,
the owners put all the houseplants
in the place (there are dozens)
up on the counter
by the big front window
where the people used to sit
with their laptops.
The plants are standing there today,
crowded together,
attentive to the light.

On a Steeple in Scaffolding

The steeple is caught in a cage of sky,
a cage of stars by night.
It stands in the skyline as something unfinished,
or finished once, to be finished once more.

The scaffold is a *midrash* on the steeple.
It makes story from discontinuities
in the structure's ascent.
It is attentive to gaps and transitions,
confiding at failures to join.
It numbers the constituent parts.

The steeple and the scaffold
are, conjoined, a moral emblem:
they are ambition regulated,
extravagance brought within bounds.
They are *semper paratus,*
or the middle way.

Substance and shadow,
the argument and the outline,
plane and surface, line and vector,
the thing itself
and the thing that itself is not:
these are held, these constitute
the cage of sky,
by night the cage of stars.

Cena Trimalchionis

The long withdrawing roar
can no longer be heard
above the small-arms fire
from the clubs
and schools
and churches.
Forests burn.
Seeds are indentured
to multinational corporations.

Of course we will be true
to one another,
but what good is truth
as Trimalchio prepares his banquet,
promises to make us great again.

President Donald J. Trump at the Western Wall, Jerusalem, 2017

The *kippah* sits as strangely
on the artifact hair
as the look of reverence
on the features
lapsed and porcine.

His hands are on
the ancient stones,
his mind on
the photographers,
perhaps.

His Israel is not a country
on the map;
it is the adjunct
to a fantasy,
a figment
of his base.

There were only
two words
on the folded note
the President placed,

beyond the camera's reach,
in a crevice of the wall.
To the God of the Patriarchs,
the Shield of Abraham,
Trump wrote:
Believe me.

The Fraying of the Flag

Over time and under
the repetitive stress
of flap and wave,
of flaunt, brandish,
and signify,
a small parting
will open in the fabric,
or in the fabric
an opening will part
as the flag rides the sky
or accommodates the wind
and over time
the parting will extend
into a tear or rent
as if the flag
were mourning itself,
rending the garment
that is itself,
and when the rent reaches
the back seam
it is no longer a flag
that flies,
but the banners
of two minor nations.

Culture Clash at the Sausage Factory

Ever since they put in the spectators' gallery,
things haven't been the same here.

Our suppliers have grown circumspect
and arrive now only in darkness.

Citing pangs of conscience,
some of our best hands have given notice.

Efficiency is down; workplace accidents are up,
and a certain *esprit de corps* has been lost.

There is no question:
transparency has been bad for business.

Profiles Theater Shuttered, June 8, 2016

After a long investigation
The Chicago Reader breaks the story
about abuse and intimidation
of women actors at Profiles Theater.
48 hours later artist-activists
cover the theater doors
with copies of the exposé.
Six days after that Profiles
closes permanently.

Truc Lam Temple Closed and Tagged

Truc Lam Buddhist Temple at Wilson and Ashland
stands empty now, having been sold for condos.

It is needless to think what shadows fall
where the people once gathered,

needless to think what has fled
the empty sanctuary.

Do not consider how taggers have marked
the plywood that seals the empty windows.

For this is consistent with the teaching:
the tags and the taggers are empty,

their colors and characters empty:
NUKEY is empty; K-9 is empty.

CORNBREAD is empty.
Needless to think.

Liu Dan, "The Dictionary," 1991, Ink and Watercolor on Paper

The painting hangs in the corridor
between Prints and Drawings,
and the Alsdorf Gallery of Asian Antiquities.
But it is also true that the corridor
hangs in the painting
along with drawings and prints,
and many other things antique and Asian.
A vast creature has been swallowed
by a creature more vast.
The painting contains the dictionary;
the dictionary contains the world.

Zen and the Music of Earth Wind and Fire

When things weren't going well
in the studio
and the fellows
were getting discouraged,
Maurice would say:
"Before enlightenment
cut wood and carry water;
after enlightenment
cut wood and carry water."

Philip might begin a session
with remarks about
how all music is supported by silence,
carries silence at its center,
and how we as musicians
must remember
that the music
is as empty
as the silence.

Verdine, more advanced
than any of them,
would gaze upon
the glass of the booth
as if the moon's face
had come to rest there.

Minor White in Love

"Have you ever been in love?"
Stieglitz asked when he met White in '46,
a questing acolyte with doubts of his vocation.
When the young man said yes,
the master replied, "then you can photograph."
That stayed with White until the end,
made articulate in him something
that had been there, silent, all along:
the knowledge that desire was an aperture
that admitted the visible world,
admitted its delectable surfaces,
bathed them in ennobling light.

The visible world provoked desire
and desire exposed the world.

White had been, would stay, in love:
with men and boys, students and strangers,
the ghost of Walt Whitman a time or two,
with the grain of wood, frost on the pane,
with paper's pucker and peel.

To be open to these,
follow to them his desire—
this would be his work.

Mr. Peale's Illustrious Sons

Rubens went in with Rembrandt
on the Baltimore place,
sold it to Barnum in the '37 panic.
Rubens thought himself
the least of the Peales:
a maker of workman-like landscapes.
Rembrandt's portrait of Rubens,
posed with a geranium
and wearing the family spectacles,
suggests a spirit inward and irresolute.

Titian, the youngest,
saw the Rockies in 1819
as assistant to Say
on Long's Yellowstone trek.
Illustrator for Say's *Entomology*
and Bonaparte's *Birds*,
author of a treatise on the preservation
of natural history collections,
Titian was the Peale
of the Peale box;
in thousands of these
he left the Academy
his butterflies and moths.

Raphael who appears
with the four-year old Titian
in their father's "Staircase Group,"
excelled at *trompe l'oeil*,
and died at 51 either
(there is controversy)

from madness and drink
or exposure to the arsenic and mercury
with which he prepared
his taxidermy specimens.
Raphael played five musical instruments,
invented a mechanical process
for drawing silhouettes,
restored an heirloom mount
of the Lewisburg bison (shot 1801),
then turned in his last terrible years
to still-lifes and miniatures.

Rembrandt was all fluency and dash,
restless with a comprehensive eye.
To London after West,
Paris after David,
then chased for twenty years
the standard likeness of *Pater Patriae*.
When Brady photographed him in 1859
Rembrandt was the only living painter
to have seen Washington.

More Archaic Torso

"Tighten Up" by Archie Bell and the Drells
tells me I must change my life.

Rousseau's "Tiger in Rain Jungle"
tells me I must change my life.

Woody Guthrie's "Talking Dust Bowl Blues"
Common's "Thelonious,"
Portrait of a Lady all tell me I must change my life.

The Picasso in Daley Plaza
tells me I must change my life.

"Wichita Vortex Sutra"
tells me I must change my life.

Turner's "Burning of the Houses of Parliament"
tells me I must change my life.

Hopper's "New York Movie"
tells me I must change my life.

Environmental Studies

We drive all night in two college vans,
west through Roundup-Ready corn and soy,
crossing at Council Bluffs into CAFO country.
The students don't seem to mind the long drive.
There is good signal on the interstate:
they YikYak and Snapchat,
microblog and game.
At dawn from a bridge over the Platte River
we watch ten-thousand cranes
rise screaming into a sunrise of blood.
The students are impressed,
they hold up their phones.

George Perkins Marsh on the Anthropogenic Dispersion of Seed

George Perkins Marsh, *Man and Nature: Or, Physical Geography as Modified by Human Action*, New York: Charles Scribner, 1864, p. 62.

In the campaign of 1814,
the Russian troops brought,
in the stuffing of their
saddles and by other

accidental means, seeds from
the banks of the Dnieper to the
valley of the Rhine, and even
introduced the plants of the steppes

into the environs of Paris. The
Turkish armies, in their incursions
into Europe, brought Eastern vegetables
on their train, and left the seeds

of Oriental wall plants to grow
upon the ramparts of Buda
and Vienna. The Canada thistle,
Erigeron canadense, is said to

have sprung up in Europe,
two hundred years ago,
from a seed which dropped
out of the stuffed skin of a bird.

Green Men

This one refuses to drink
privatized water,
and packs in
city tap,
which he husbands,
self-cherishingly,
until he finds
a seep, spring,
or sink.

Another will hear
no music
on a platform
that returns royalties,
plays unsigned mixtapes
when he drives you
to the backcountry.

Here's one who claims
to have caught
a Rufous Hummingbird
in a snare
of filament and picture wire.
That was in his wild days,
he tells you,
before he came here
for his degree.

Marked Animals

In one of the northern-tier counties of Wisconsin
Indigenous people in the Russian arctic
hunters reported a white-tailed deer,
recently caught on a cellphone video
a second-year spike-horn buck, they said,
a Polar Bear that had been spray-painted
with a high-visibility blaze-orange scarf
with large letters that read T-34
tied loosely but securely about its neck.
(the model number of an obsolete Soviet tank).
They were unable to shoot the marked animal,
Wildlife officials, reviewing the video, expressed concern
and watched it pass brightly into the woods beyond.
that the graffiti would impair the bear's ability to hunt.

Googling the Dead

It seems at first like a way of keeping them,
of giving them a place in the here and now
you may pretend not to know they have lost.
They can be in this way more quick than dead,
their results robust, their vitals still vital.
And you may fool yourself in this way,
until their footprint contracts, sites shut down
or update, the algorithm moves on,
and your dead retreat once more,
a little further away.

National Prose Month

During National Prose Month
we will sit in even rows
and dedicate ourselves
to lucid exposition.

We will offer an unambiguous thesis
and refer to it frequently
in a defense rich with
concrete examples.

Assonance and consonance
will be discouraged.
The chromatic and the lyrical
will be disallowed.

Purple may be applied sparingly
during National Prose Month,
but there will be none of
that Aeolian business, please.

I personally will hang my hat
upon this bust of Cicero
that keeps my desk anchored
firmly to the ground.

In the Hebrew Cemetery of Sheboygan

Mr. Kohler, the plumbing-fixtures magnate,
bought the land for the congregation
in the early days of the last century.
The graves now stand across the road
from the great resort that
blesses his name.

There the elite and would-be meet to golf,
the forces of sales retreat
to PowerPoint and pork-wrapped dates
in a suite of conference rooms
themed Great Lakes:
Traverse Bay,
Sister Bay.

But here the Hebrews sleep like corn in rows.
It is midwestern August:
the cricket dithers,
the cicada cannot come to the point,
and thunderstorm is latent in the afternoon air.
This is the celebrated sleep of the just.

These Jews were glacial erratics.
Latecomers and outliers to the tribe at Milwaukee,
they came to rest sixty miles north on the littoral moraine.
They were Litvaks, Belaruskis from Vitebsk and Mir,
their Europe unimaginable from here and now.
They came for jobs with Mr. Kohler.

Here in Sheboygan they labored and prayed,
suffered exclusion or didn't,
prospered or not,
and went to sleep beneath
this immaculate lawn.

Now only the lawn guys visit the Hebrew cemetery.
The synagogues in town were long ago converted,
and no one has been buried here in thirty years.
You would think the Jews had given up dying.

As the poets have reported
from other localities,
the Jews have disappeared from Sheboygan.
Gone from Redwing and Deer Gaze,
gone from Kiwanis Park.
The Objibwe are not more scarce
on this lakeshore than the Jews.

As with the glacier,
we may infer something of them
from their absence,
from what they shaped and touched,
from the course of their drift.
Perhaps a descendent,
untouched by the past that sleeps here,
sometimes golfs at Kohler's resort.

Couple-Shtick

There is for example the running bit
about the laundry:
how there is the laundry of color,
the laundry that thinks it is white,
and the laundry that is thermo-atypical.

Or if you say "Chisholm Trail emotion"
I know you're talking about
how the Kevin Bacon character feels
in Barry Levinson's *Diner*
when the aristo girl on the horse
tells him her name.

When I speak certain words
that scan dactyl trochee
like buffalo soldier,
you are likely to holler back
from "Buffalo Soldier."

It is liturgy, freemasonry,
it is Operator's Manual.
On we go through the years.

On the Persistence of the Self

It is almost certainly a trick of the brain:
the neurons build an effigy
in which the body invests.
Or perhaps it is the creation of time itself,
a looking-glass in which the years
mug and grimace, watching themselves go by.
A narrative, a *trompe l'oeil,*
a grinning Kabuki mask
to which we cleave like flesh to bone.

Yet as the old man steps outside
this first evening of frost
it is the boy who smells the wood smoke on the air.
The boy is a fly in amber.
The boy is a prisoner of memory.
The boy is a project of the mind.

At Ausfess castle, ancestral seat
of his mother's family, the von Rankes,
Robert Graves found among the family treasures:
"A wine glass that my uncle's old father,
the reigning baron,
had found in the Franco-Prussian war
standing upright
in the middle of the square
of an entirely ruined village."

Glossary of Yiddish Terms

Alrightniks: successful, prosperous Jews. Those who had done "all right" in America.
Chazerei: junk, trash. Literally, stuff for pigs.
Europsche: European.
Farklempt: choked up
Farshimmelt: messy, disorderly. Literally, decayed or moldy.
Feh: expression of disgust.
Frummer: a pious or observant Jew.
Gesheft: business.
Mamaloshen: Yiddish. Literally, mother tongue.
Putz: vulgar word for penis.
Shtetl: little European village.
Tante: aunt.
Tateleh: affectionate diminutive for father.
Treyf: unkosher.
Yiddishkeit: the culture of Yiddish-speaking communities.

About the Author

Benjamin Goluboff is the author of *Ho Chi Minh: A Speculative Life in Verse* (Urban Farmhouse Press) and, in collaboration with the Massachusetts poet Mark Luebbers, *Group Portrait: Poems on a Photography by Herman Landshoff* (Parisian Phoenix). Goluboff teaches in the English Department at Lake Forest College; his work is easy to find on the internet.

www.ingramcontent.com/pod-product-compliance
Lightning Source LLC
Chambersburg PA
CBHW072200160426
43197CB00012B/2470